KU-686-312

INTRODUCTORY NOTE

JEAN BAPTISTE RACINE, the younger contemporary of Corneille, and his rival for supremacy in French classical tragedy, was born at Ferte- Milon, December 21, 1639. He was educated at the College of Beauvais, at the great Jansenist school at Port Royal, and at the College d'Harcourt. He attracted notice by an ode written for the marriage of Louis XIV in 1660, and made his first really great dramatic success with his "Andromaque. " His tragic masterpieces include "Britannicus, " "Berenice, " "Bajazet, " "Mithridate, " "Iphigenie, " and "Phaedre, " all written between 1669 and 1677. Then for some years he gave up dramatic composition, disgusted by the intrigues of enemies who sought to injure his career by exalting above him an unworthy rival. In 1689 he resumed his work under the persuasion of Mme. de Maintenon, and produced "Esther" and "Athalie, " the latter ranking among his finest productions, although it did not receive public recognition until some time after his death in 1699. Besides his tragedies, Racine wrote one comedy, "Les Plaideurs, " four hymns of great beauty, and a history of Port Royal.

The external conventions of classical tragedy which had been established by Corneille, Racine did not attempt to modify. His study of the Greek tragedians and his own taste led him to submit willingly to the rigor and simplicity of form which were the fundamental marks of the classical ideal. It was in his treatment of character that he differed most from his predecessor; for whereas, as we have seen, Corneille represented his leading figures as heroically subduing passion by force of will, Racine represents his as driven by almost uncontrollable passion. Thus his creations appeal to the modern reader as more warmly human; their speech, if less exalted, is simpler and more natural; and he succeeds more brilliantly with his portraits of women than with those of men.

All these characteristics are exemplified in "Phaedre, " the tragedy of Racine which has made an appeal to the widest audience. To the legend as treated by Euripides, Racine added the love of Hippolytus for Aricia, and thus supplied a motive for Phaedra's jealousy, and at the same time he made the nurse instead of Phaedra the calumniator of his son to Theseus.

CHARACTERS

THESEUS, son of Aegeus and King of Athens.
PHAEDRA, wife of Theseus and Daughter of Minos and Pasiphae.
HIPPOLYTUS, son of Theseus and Antiope, Queen of the Amazons.
ARICIA, Princess of the Blood Royal of Athens.
OENONE, nurse of Phaedra.
THERAMENES, tutor of Hippolytus.
ISMENE, bosom friend of Aricia.
PANOPE, waiting-woman of Phaedra.
GUARDS.

The scene is laid at Troezen, a town of the Peloponnesus

Phaedra

ACT I

SCENE I
HIPPOLYTUS, THERAMENES

HIPPOLYTUS
My mind is settled, dear Theramenes,
And I can stay no more in lovely Troezen.
In doubt that racks my soul with mortal anguish,
I grow ashamed of such long idleness.
Six months and more my father has been gone,
And what may have befallen one so dear
I know not, nor what corner of the earth
Hides him.

THERAMENES
And where, prince, will you look for him?
Already, to content your just alarm,
Have I not cross'd the seas on either side
Of Corinth, ask'd if aught were known of Theseus
Where Acheron is lost among the Shades,
Visited Elis, doubled Toenarus,
And sail'd into the sea that saw the fall
Of Icarus? Inspired with what new hope,
Under what favour'd skies think you to trace
His footsteps? Who knows if the King, your father,
Wishes the secret of his absence known?
Perchance, while we are trembling for his life,
The hero calmly plots some fresh intrigue,
And only waits till the deluded fair—

HIPPOLYTUS
Cease, dear Theramenes, respect the name
Of Theseus. Youthful errors have been left
Behind, and no unworthy obstacle
Detains him. Phaedra long has fix'd a heart
Inconstant once, nor need she fear a rival.
In seeking him I shall but do my duty,
And leave a place I dare no longer see.

THERAMENES
Indeed! When, prince, did you begin to dread
These peaceful haunts, so dear to happy childhood,
Where I have seen you oft prefer to stay,
Rather than meet the tumult and the pomp
Of Athens and the court? What danger shun you,
Or shall I say what grief?

HIPPOLYTUS
That happy time
Is gone, and all is changed, since to these shores
The gods sent Phaedra.

THERAMENES
I perceive the cause
Of your distress. It is the queen whose sight
Offends you. With a step-dame's spite she schemed
Your exile soon as she set eyes on you.
But if her hatred is not wholly vanish'd,
It has at least taken a milder aspect.
Besides, what danger can a dying woman,
One too who longs for death, bring on your head?
Can Phaedra, sick'ning of a dire disease
Of which she will not speak, weary of life
And of herself, form any plots against you?

HIPPOLYTUS
It is not her vain enmity I fear,
Another foe alarms Hippolytus.
I fly, it must be own'd, from young Aricia,
The sole survivor of an impious race.

THERAMENES
What! You become her persecutor too!
The gentle sister of the cruel sons
Of Pallas shared not in their perfidy;
Why should you hate such charming innocence?

HIPPOLYTUS
I should not need to fly, if it were hatred.

THERAMENES
May I, then, learn the meaning of your flight?

2

Phaedra

Is this the proud Hippolytus I see,
Than whom there breathed no fiercer foe to love
And to that yoke which Theseus has so oft
Endured? And can it be that Venus, scorn'd
So long, will justify your sire at last?
Has she, then, setting you with other mortals,
Forced e'en Hippolytus to offer incense
Before her? Can you love?

HIPPOLYTUS
Friend, ask me not.
You, who have known my heart from infancy
And all its feelings of disdainful pride,
Spare me the shame of disavowing all
That I profess'd. Born of an Amazon,
The wildness that you wonder at I suck'd
With mother's milk. When come to riper age,
Reason approved what Nature had implanted.
Sincerely bound to me by zealous service,
You told me then the story of my sire,
And know how oft, attentive to your voice,
I kindled when I heard his noble acts,
As you described him bringing consolation
To mortals for the absence of Alcides,
The highways clear'd of monsters and of robbers,
Procrustes, Cercyon, Sciro, Sinnis slain,
The Epidaurian giant's bones dispersed,
Crete reeking with the blood of Minotaur.
But when you told me of less glorious deeds,
Troth plighted here and there and everywhere,
Young Helen stolen from her home at Sparta,
And Periboea's tears in Salamis,
With many another trusting heart deceived
Whose very names have 'scaped his memory,
Forsaken Ariadne to the rocks
Complaining, last this Phaedra, bound to him
By better ties, —you know with what regret
I heard and urged you to cut short the tale,
Happy had I been able to erase
From my remembrance that unworthy part
Of such a splendid record. I, in turn,
Am I too made the slave of love, and brought
To stoop so low? The more contemptible

That no renown is mine such as exalts
The name of Theseus, that no monsters quell'd
Have given me a right to share his weakness.
And if my pride of heart must needs be humbled,
Aricia should have been the last to tame it.
Was I beside myself to have forgotten
Eternal barriers of separation
Between us? By my father's stern command
Her brethren's blood must ne'er be reinforced
By sons of hers; he dreads a single shoot
From stock so guilty, and would fain with her
Bury their name, that, even to the tomb
Content to be his ward, for her no torch
Of Hymen may be lit. Shall I espouse
Her rights against my sire, rashly provoke
His wrath, and launch upon a mad career—

THERAMENES
The gods, dear prince, if once your hour is come,
Care little for the reasons that should guide us.
Wishing to shut your eyes, Theseus unseals them;
His hatred, stirring a rebellious flame
Within you, lends his enemy new charms.
And, after all, why should a guiltless passion
Alarm you? Dare you not essay its sweetness,
But follow rather a fastidious scruple?
Fear you to stray where Hercules has wander'd?
What heart so stout that Venus has not vanquish'd?
Where would you be yourself, so long her foe,
Had your own mother, constant in her scorn
Of love, ne'er glowed with tenderness for Theseus?
What boots it to affect a pride you feel not?
Confess it, all is changed; for some time past
You have been seldom seen with wild delight
Urging the rapid car along the strand,
Or, skilful in the art that Neptune taught,
Making th' unbroken steed obey the bit;
Less often have the woods return'd our shouts;
A secret burden on your spirits cast
Has dimm'd your eye. How can I doubt you love?
Vainly would you conceal the fatal wound.
Has not the fair Aricia touch'd your heart?

HIPPOLYTUS
Theramenes, I go to find my father.

THERAMENES
Will you not see the queen before you start,
My prince?

HIPPOLYTUS
That is my purpose: you can tell her.
Yes, I will see her; duty bids me do it.
But what new ill vexes her dear Oenone?

SCENE II
HIPPOLYTUS, OENONE, THERAMENES

OENONE
Alas, my lord, what grief was e'er like mine?
The queen has almost touch'd the gates of death.
Vainly close watch I keep by day and night,
E'en in my arms a secret malady
Slays her, and all her senses are disorder'd.
Weary yet restless from her couch she rises,
Pants for the outer air, but bids me see
That no one on her misery intrudes.
She comes.

HIPPOLYTUS
Enough. She shall not be disturb'd,
Nor be confronted with a face she hates.

SCENE III
PHAEDRA, OENONE

PHAEDRA
We have gone far enough. Stay, dear Oenone;
Strength fails me, and I needs must rest awhile.
My eyes are dazzled with this glaring light
So long unseen, my trembling knees refuse
Support. Ah me!

OENONE
Would Heaven that our tears
Might bring relief!

PHAEDRA
Ah, how these cumbrous gauds,
These veils oppress me! What officious hand
Has tied these knots, and gather'd o'er my brow
These clustering coils? How all conspires to add
To my distress!

OENONE
What is one moment wish'd,
The next, is irksome. Did you not just now,
Sick of inaction, bid us deck you out,
And, with your former energy recall'd,
Desire to go abroad, and see the light
Of day once more? You see it, and would fain
Be hidden from the sunshine that you sought.

PHAEDRA
Thou glorious author of a hapless race,
Whose daughter 'twas my mother's boast to be,
Who well may'st blush to see me in such plight,
For the last time I come to look on thee,
O Sun!

OENONE
What! Still are you in love with death?
Shall I ne'er see you, reconciled to life,
Forego these cruel accents of despair?

PHAEDRA
Would I were seated in the forest's shade!
When may I follow with delighted eye,
Thro' glorious dust flying in full career,
A chariot—

OENONE
Madam?

PHAEDRA
Have I lost my senses?
What said I? and where am I? Whither stray
Vain wishes? Ah! The gods have made me mad.
I blush, Oenone, and confusion covers
My face, for I have let you see too clearly
The shame of grief that, in my own despite,
O'erflows these eyes of mine.

OENONE
If you must blush,
Blush at a silence that inflames your woes.
Resisting all my care, deaf to my voice,
Will you have no compassion on yourself,
But let your life be ended in mid course?
What evil spell has drain'd its fountain dry?
Thrice have the shades of night obscured the heav'ns
Since sleep has enter'd thro' your eyes, and thrice
The dawn has chased the darkness thence, since food
Pass'd your wan lips, and you are faint and languid.
To what dread purpose is your heart inclined?
How dare you make attempts upon your life,
And so offend the gods who gave it you,
Prove false to Theseus and your marriage vows,
Ay, and betray your most unhappy children,
Bending their necks yourself beneath the yoke?
That day, be sure, which robs them of their mother,
Will give high hopes back to the stranger's son,
To that proud enemy of you and yours,
To whom an Amazon gave birth, I mean
Hippolytus—

PHAEDRA
Ye gods!

8

OENONE
Ah, this reproach
Moves you!

PHAEDRA
Unhappy woman, to what name
Gave your mouth utterance?

OENONE
Your wrath is just.
'Tis well that that ill-omen'd name can rouse
Such rage. Then live. Let love and duty urge
Their claims. Live, suffer not this son of Scythia,
Crushing your children 'neath his odious sway,
To rule the noble offspring of the gods,
The purest blood of Greece. Make no delay;
Each moment threatens death; quickly restore
Your shatter'd strength, while yet the torch of life
Holds out, and can be fann'd into a flame.

PHAEDRA
Too long have I endured its guilt and shame!

OENONE
Why? What remorse gnaws at your heart? What crime
Can have disturb'd you thus? Your hands are not
Polluted with the blood of innocence?

PHAEDRA
Thanks be to Heav'n, my hands are free from stain.
Would that my soul were innocent as they!

OENONE
What awful project have you then conceived,
Whereat your conscience should be still alarm'd?

PHAEDRA
Have I not said enough? Spare me the rest.
I die to save myself a full confession.

OENONE
Die then, and keep a silence so inhuman;
But seek some other hand to close your eyes.

Tho' but a spark of life remains within you,
My soul shall go before you to the Shades.
A thousand roads are always open thither;
Pain'd at your want of confidence, I'll choose
The shortest. Cruel one, when has my faith
Deceived you! Think how in my arms you lay
New born. For you, my country and my children
I have forsaken. Do you thus repay
My faithful service?

PHAEDRA
What do you expect
From words so bitter? Were I to break silence
Horror would freeze your blood.

OENONE
What can you say
To horrify me more than to behold
You die before my eyes?

PHAEDRA
When you shall know
My crime, my death will follow none the less,
But with the added stain of guilt.

OENONE
Dear Madam,
By all the tears that I have shed for you,
By these weak knees I clasp, relieve my mind
From torturing doubt.

PHAEDRA
It is your wish. Then rise.

OENONE
I hear you. Speak.

PHAEDRA
Heav'ns! How shall I begin?

OENONE
Dismiss vain fears, you wound me with distrust.

Phaedra

PHAEDRA
O fatal animosity of Venus!
Into what wild distractions did she cast
My mother!

OENONE
Be they blotted from remembrance,
And for all time to come buried in silence.

PHAEDRA
My sister Ariadne, by what love
Were you betray'd to death, on lonely shores
Forsaken!

OENONE
Madam, what deep-seated pain
Prompts these reproaches against all your kin?

PHAEDRA
It is the will of Venus, and I perish,
Last, most unhappy of a family
Where all were wretched.

OENONE
Do you love?

PHAEDRA
I feel
All its mad fever.

OENONE
Ah! For whom?

PHAEDRA
Hear now
The crowning horror. Yes, I love—my lips
Tremble to say his name.

OENONE
Whom?

PHAEDRA
Know you him,

Phaedra

Son of the Amazon, whom I've oppress'd
So long?

OENONE
Hippolytus? Great gods!

PHAEDRA
'Tis you
Have named him.

OENONE
All my blood within my veins
Seems frozen. O despair! O cursed race!
Ill-omen'd journey! Land of misery!
Why did we ever reach thy dangerous shores?

PHAEDRA
My wound is not so recent. Scarcely had I
Been bound to Theseus by the marriage yoke,
And happiness and peace seem'd well secured,
When Athens show'd me my proud enemy.
I look'd, alternately turn'd pale and blush'd
To see him, and my soul grew all distraught;
A mist obscured my vision, and my voice
Falter'd, my blood ran cold, then burn'd like fire;
Venus I felt in all my fever'd frame,
Whose fury had so many of my race
Pursued. With fervent vows I sought to shun
Her torments, built and deck'd for her a shrine,
And there, 'mid countless victims did I seek
The reason I had lost; but all for naught,
No remedy could cure the wounds of love!
In vain I offer'd incense on her altars;
When I invoked her name my heart adored
Hippolytus, before me constantly;
And when I made her altars smoke with victims,
'Twas for a god whose name I dared not utter.
I fled his presence everywhere, but found him—
O crowning horror! —in his father's features.
Against myself, at last, I raised revolt,
And stirr'd my courage up to persecute
The enemy I loved. To banish him
I wore a step—dame's harsh and jealous carriage,

12

Phaedra

With ceaseless cries I clamour'd for his exile,
Till I had torn him from his father's arms.
I breathed once more, Oenone; in his absence
My days flow'd on less troubled than before,
And innocent. Submissive to my husband,
I hid my grief, and of our fatal marriage
Cherish'd the fruits. Vain caution! Cruel Fate!
Brought hither by my spouse himself, I saw
Again the enemy whom I had banish'd,
And the old wound too quickly bled afresh.
No longer is it love hid in my heart,
But Venus in her might seizing her prey.
I have conceived just terror for my crime;
I hate my life, and hold my love in horror.
Dying I wish'd to keep my fame unsullied,
And bury in the grave a guilty passion;
But I have been unable to withstand
Tears and entreaties, I have told you all;
Content, if only, as my end draws near,
You do not vex me with unjust reproaches,
Nor with vain efforts seek to snatch from death
The last faint lingering sparks of vital breath.

SCENE IV
PHAEDRA, OENONE, PANOPE

PANOPE
Fain would I hide from you tidings so sad,
But 'tis my duty, Madam, to reveal them.
The hand of death has seized your peerless husband,
And you are last to hear of this disaster.

OENONE
What say you, Panope?

PANOPE
The queen, deceived
By a vain trust in Heav'n, begs safe return
For Theseus, while Hippolytus his son
Learns of his death from vessels that are now
In port.

PHAEDRA
Ye gods!

PANOPE
Divided counsels sway
The choice of Athens; some would have the prince,
Your child, for master; others, disregarding
The laws, dare to support the stranger's son.
'Tis even said that a presumptuous faction
Would crown Aricia and the house of Pallas.
I deem'd it right to warn you of this danger.
Hippolytus already is prepared
To start, and should he show himself at Athens,
'Tis to be fear'd the fickle crowd will all
Follow his lead.

OENONE
Enough. The queen, who hears you,
By no means will neglect this timely warning.

SCENE V
PHAEDRA, OENONE

OENONE

Dear lady, I had almost ceased to urge
The wish that you should live, thinking to follow
My mistress to the tomb, from which my voice
Had fail'd to turn you; but this new misfortune
Alters the aspect of affairs, and prompts
Fresh measures. Madam, Theseus is no more,
You must supply his place. He leaves a son,
A slave, if you should die, but, if you live,
A King. On whom has he to lean but you?
No hand but yours will dry his tears. Then live
For him, or else the tears of innocence
Will move the gods, his ancestors, to wrath
Against his mother. Live, your guilt is gone,
No blame attaches to your passion now.
The King's decease has freed you from the bonds
That made the crime and horror of your love.
Hippolytus no longer need be dreaded,
Him you may see henceforth without reproach.
It may be, that, convinced of your aversion,
He means to head the rebels. Undeceive him,
Soften his callous heart, and bend his pride.
King of this fertile land, in Troezen here
His portion lies; but as he knows, the laws
Give to your son the ramparts that Minerva
Built and protects. A common enemy
Threatens you both, unite them to oppose
Aricia.

PHAEDRA

To your counsel I consent.
Yes, I will live, if life can be restored,
If my affection for a son has pow'r
To rouse my sinking heart at such a dangerous hour.

ACT II

SCENE I
ARICIA, ISMENE

ARICIA
Hippolytus request to see me here!
Hippolytus desire to bid farewell!
Is't true, Ismene? Are you not deceived?

ISMENE
This is the first result of Theseus' death.
Prepare yourself to see from every side.
Hearts turn towards you that were kept away
By Theseus. Mistress of her lot at last,
Aricia soon shall find all Greece fall low,
To do her homage.

ARICIA
'Tis not then, Ismene,
An idle tale? Am I no more a slave?
Have I no enemies?

ISMENE
The gods oppose
Your peace no longer, and the soul of Theseus
Is with your brothers.

ARICIA
Does the voice of fame
Tell how he died?

ISMENE
Rumours incredible
Are spread. Some say that, seizing a new bride,
The faithless husband by the waves was swallow'd.
Others affirm, and this report prevails,
That with Pirithous to the world below
He went, and saw the shores of dark Cocytus,
Showing himself alive to the pale ghosts;

16

But that he could not leave those gloomy realms,
Which whoso enters there abides for ever.

ARICIA
Shall I believe that ere his destined hour
A mortal may descend into the gulf
Of Hades? What attraction could o'ercome
Its terrors?

ISMENE
He is dead, and you alone
Doubt it. The men of Athens mourn his loss.
Troezen already hails Hippolytus
As King. And Phaedra, fearing for her son,
Asks counsel of the friends who share her trouble,
Here in this palace.

ARICIA
Will Hippolytus,
Think you, prove kinder than his sire, make light
My chains, and pity my misfortunes?

ISMENE
Yes,
I think so, Madam.

ARICIA
Ah, you know him not
Or you would never deem so hard a heart
Can pity feel, or me alone except
From the contempt in which he holds our sex.
Has he not long avoided every spot
Where we resort?

ISMENE
I know what tales are told
Of proud Hippolytus, but I have seen
Him near you, and have watch'd with curious eye
How one esteem'd so cold would bear himself.
Little did his behavior correspond
With what I look'd for; in his face confusion
Appear'd at your first glance, he could not turn
His languid eyes away, but gazed on you.

17

Love is a word that may offend his pride,
But what the tongue disowns, looks can betray.

ARICIA
How eagerly my heart hears what you say,
Tho' it may be delusion, dear Ismene!
Did it seem possible to you, who know me,
That I, sad sport of a relentless Fate,
Fed upon bitter tears by night and day,
Could ever taste the maddening draught of love?
The last frail offspring of a royal race,
Children of Earth, I only have survived
War's fury. Cut off in the flow'r of youth,
Mown by the sword, six brothers have I lost,
The hope of an illustrious house, whose blood
Earth drank with sorrow, near akin to his
Whom she herself produced. Since then, you know
How thro' all Greece no heart has been allow'd
To sigh for me, lest by a sister's flame
The brothers' ashes be perchance rekindled.
You know, besides, with what disdain I view'd
My conqueror's suspicions and precautions,
And how, oppos'd as I have ever been
To love, I often thank'd the King's injustice
Which happily confirm'd my inclination.
But then I never had beheld his son.
Not that, attracted merely by the eye, I
love him for his beauty and his grace,
Endowments which he owes to Nature's bounty,
Charms which he seems to know not or to scorn.
I love and prize in him riches more rare,
The virtues of his sire, without his faults.
I love, as I must own, that generous pride
Which ne'er has stoop'd beneath the amorous yoke.
Phaedra reaps little glory from a lover
So lavish of his sighs; I am too proud
To share devotion with a thousand others,
Or enter where the door is always open.
But to make one who ne'er has stoop'd before
Bend his proud neck, to pierce a heart of stone,
To bind a captive whom his chains astonish,
Who vainly 'gainst a pleasing yoke rebels, —
That piques my ardour, and I long for that.

Phaedra

'Twas easier to disarm the god of strength
Than this Hippolytus, for Hercules
Yielded so often to the eyes of beauty,
As to make triumph cheap. But, dear Ismene,
I take too little heed of opposition
Beyond my pow'r to quell, and you may hear me,
Humbled by sore defeat, upbraid the pride
I now admire. What! Can he love? and I
Have had the happiness to bend —

ISMENE
He comes
Yourself shall hear him.

SCENE II
HIPPOLYTUS, ARICIA, ISMENE

HIPPOLYTUS
Lady, ere I go
My duty bids me tell you of your change
Of fortune. My worst fears are realized;
My sire is dead. Yes, his protracted absence
Was caused as I foreboded. Death alone,
Ending his toils, could keep him from the world
Conceal'd so long. The gods at last have doom'd
Alcides' friend, companion, and successor.
I think your hatred, tender to his virtues,
Can hear such terms of praise without resentment,
Knowing them due. One hope have I that soothes
My sorrow: I can free you from restraint.
Lo, I revoke the laws whose rigour moved
My pity; you are at your own disposal,
Both heart and hand; here, in my heritage,
In Troezen, where my grandsire Pittheus reign'd
Of yore and I am now acknowledged King,
I leave you free, free as myself, —and more.

ARICIA
Your kindness is too great, 'tis overwhelming.
Such generosity, that pays disgrace
With honour, lends more force than you can think
To those harsh laws from which you would release me.

HIPPOLYTUS
Athens, uncertain how to fill the throne
Of Theseus, speaks of you, anon of me,
And then of Phaedra's son.

ARICIA
Of me, my lord?

HIPPOLYTUS
I know myself excluded by strict law:
Greece turns to my reproach a foreign mother.
But if my brother were my only rival,

My rights prevail o'er his clearly enough
To make me careless of the law's caprice.
My forwardness is check'd by juster claims:
To you I yield my place, or, rather, own
That it is yours by right, and yours the sceptre,
As handed down from Earth's great son, Erechtheus.
Adoption placed it in the hands of Aegeus:
Athens, by him protected and increased,
Welcomed a king so generous as my sire,
And left your hapless brothers in oblivion.
Now she invites you back within her walls;
Protracted strife has cost her groans enough,
Her fields are glutted with your kinsmen's blood
Fatt'ning the furrows out of which it sprung
At first. I rule this Troezen; while the son
Of Phaedra has in Crete a rich domain.
Athens is yours. I will do all I can
To join for you the votes divided now
Between us.

ARICIA
Stunn'd at all I hear, my lord,
I fear, I almost fear a dream deceives me.
Am I indeed awake? Can I believe
Such generosity? What god has put it
Into your heart? Well is the fame deserved
That you enjoy! That fame falls short of truth!
Would you for me prove traitor to yourself?
Was it not boon enough never to hate me,
So long to have abstain'd from harbouring
The enmity—

HIPPOLYTUS
To hate you? I, to hate you?
However darkly my fierce pride was painted,
Do you suppose a monster gave me birth?
What savage temper, what envenom'd hatred
Would not be mollified at sight of you?
Could I resist the soul-bewitching charm—

ARICIA
Why, what is this, Sir?

21

Phaedra

HIPPOLYTUS

I have said too much
Not to say more. Prudence in vain resists
The violence of passion. I have broken
Silence at last, and I must tell you now
The secret that my heart can hold no longer.
You see before you an unhappy instance
Of hasty pride, a prince who claims compassion
I, who, so long the enemy of Love,
Mock'd at his fetters and despised his captives,
Who, pitying poor mortals that were shipwreck'd,
In seeming safety view'd the storms from land,
Now find myself to the same fate exposed,
Toss'd to and fro upon a sea of troubles!
My boldness has been vanquish'd in a moment,
And humbled is the pride wherein I boasted.
For nearly six months past, ashamed, despairing,
Bearing where'er I go the shaft that rends
My heart, I struggle vainly to be free
From you and from myself; I shun you, present;
Absent, I find you near; I see your form
In the dark forest depths; the shades of night,
Nor less broad daylight, bring back to my view
The charms that I avoid; all things conspire
To make Hippolytus your slave. For fruit
Of all my bootless sighs, I fail to find
My former self. My bow and javelins
Please me no more, my chariot is forgotten,
With all the Sea God's lessons; and the woods
Echo my groans instead of joyous shouts
Urging my fiery steeds.

Hearing this tale
Of passion so uncouth, you blush perchance
At your own handiwork. With what wild words
I offer you my heart, strange captive held
By silken jess! But dearer in your eyes
Should be the offering, that this language comes
Strange to my lips; reject not vows express'd
So ill, which but for you had ne'er been form'd.

SCENE III
HIPPOLYTUS, ARICIA, THERAMENES, ISMENE

THERAMENES
Prince, the Queen comes. I herald her approach.
'Tis you she seeks.

HIPPOLYTUS
Me?

THERAMENES
What her thought may be
I know not. But I speak on her behalf.
She would converse with you ere you go hence.

HIPPOLYTUS
What shall I say to her? Can she expect —

ARICIA
You cannot, noble Prince, refuse to hear her,
Howe'er convinced she is your enemy,
Some shade of pity to her tears is due.

HIPPOLYTUS
Shall we part thus? and will you let me go,
Not knowing if my boldness has offended
The goddess I adore? Whether this heart,
Left in your hands —

ARICIA
Go, Prince, pursue the schemes
Your generous soul dictates, make Athens own
My sceptre. All the gifts you offer me
Will I accept, but this high throne of empire
Is not the one most precious in my sight.

SCENE IV
HIPPOLYTUS, THERAMENES

HIPPOLYTUS
Friend, is all ready?
But the Queen approaches.
Go, see the vessel in fit trim to sail.
Haste, bid the crew aboard, and hoist the signal:
Then soon return, and so deliver me
From interview most irksome.

Phaedra

SCENE V
PHAEDRA, HIPPOLYTUS, OENONE

PHAEDRA (to OENONE)
There I see him!
My blood forgets to flow, my tongue to speak
What I am come to say.

OENONE
Think of your son,
How all his hopes depend on you.

PHAEDRA
I hear
You leave us, and in haste. I come to add
My tears to your distress, and for a son
Plead my alarm. No more has he a father,
And at no distant day my son must witness
My death. Already do a thousand foes
Threaten his youth. You only can defend him
But in my secret heart remorse awakes,
And fear lest I have shut your ears against
His cries. I tremble lest your righteous anger
Visit on him ere long the hatred earn'd
By me, his mother.

HIPPOLYTUS
No such base resentment,
Madam, is mine.

PHAEDRA
I could not blame you, Prince,
If you should hate me. I have injured you:
So much you know, but could not read my heart.
T' incur your enmity has been mine aim.
The self-same borders could not hold us both;
In public and in private I declared
Myself your foe, and found no peace till seas
Parted us from each other. I forbade
Your very name to be pronounced before me.
And yet if punishment should be proportion'd

25

Phaedra

To the offence, if only hatred draws
Your hatred, never woman merited
More pity, less deserved your enmity.

HIPPOLYTUS
A mother jealous of her children's rights
Seldom forgives the offspring of a wife
Who reign'd before her. Harassing suspicions
Are common sequels of a second marriage.
Of me would any other have been jealous
No less than you, perhaps more violent.

PHAEDRA
Ah, Prince, how Heav'n has from the general law
Made me exempt, be that same Heav'n my witness!
Far different is the trouble that devours me!

HIPPOLYTUS
This is no time for self-reproaches, Madam.
It may be that your husband still beholds
The light, and Heav'n may grant him safe return,
In answer to our prayers. His guardian god
Is Neptune, ne'er by him invoked in vain.

PHAEDRA
He who has seen the mansions of the dead
Returns not thence. Since to those gloomy shores
Theseus is gone, 'tis vain to hope that Heav'n
May send him back. Prince, there is no release
From Acheron's greedy maw. And yet, methinks,
He lives, and breathes in you. I see him still
Before me, and to him I seem to speak;
My heart—
Oh! I am mad; do what I will,
I cannot hide my passion.

HIPPOLYTUS
Yes, I see
The strange effects of love. Theseus, tho' dead,
Seems present to your eyes, for in your soul
There burns a constant flame.

Phaedra

PHAEDRA
Ah, yes for Theseus
I languish and I long, not as the Shades
Have seen him, of a thousand different forms
The fickle lover, and of Pluto's bride
The would-be ravisher, but faithful, proud
E'en to a slight disdain, with youthful charms
Attracting every heart, as gods are painted,
Or like yourself. He had your mien, your eyes,
Spoke and could blush like you, when to the isle
Of Crete, my childhood's home, he cross'd the waves,
Worthy to win the love of Minos' daughters.
What were you doing then? Why did he gather
The flow'r of Greece, and leave Hippolytus?
Oh, why were you too young to have embark'd
On board the ship that brought thy sire to Crete?
At your hands would the monster then have perish'd,
Despite the windings of his vast retreat.
To guide your doubtful steps within the maze
My sister would have arm'd you with the clue.
But no, therein would Phaedra have forestall'd her,
Love would have first inspired me with the thought;
And I it would have been whose timely aid
Had taught you all the labyrinth's crooked ways.
What anxious care a life so dear had cost me!
No thread had satisfied your lover's fears:
I would myself have wish'd to lead the way,
And share the peril you were bound to face;
Phaedra with you would have explored the maze,
With you emerged in safety, or have perish'd.

HIPPOLYTUS
Gods! What is this I hear? Have you forgotten
That Theseus is my father and your husband?

PHAEDRA
Why should you fancy I have lost remembrance
Thereof, and am regardless of mine honour?

HIPPOLYTUS
Forgive me, Madam. With a blush I own
That I misconstrued words of innocence.
For very shame I cannot bear your sight

Longer. I go—
PHAEDRA
Ah! cruel Prince, too well
You understood me. I have said enough
To save you from mistake. I love. But think not
That at the moment when I love you most
I do not feel my guilt; no weak compliance
Has fed the poison that infects my brain.
The ill-starr'd object of celestial vengeance,
I am not so detestable to you
As to myself. The gods will bear me witness,
Who have within my veins kindled this fire,
The gods, who take a barbarous delight
In leading a poor mortal's heart astray.
Do you yourself recall to mind the past:
'Twas not enough for me to fly, I chased you
Out of the country, wishing to appear
Inhuman, odious; to resist you better,
I sought to make you hate me. All in vain!
Hating me more I loved you none the less:
New charms were lent to you by your misfortunes.
I have been drown'd in tears, and scorch'd by fire;
Your own eyes might convince you of the truth,
If for one moment you could look at me.
What is't I say? Think you this vile confession
That I have made is what I meant to utter?
Not daring to betray a son for whom
I trembled, 'twas to beg you not to hate him
I came. Weak purpose of a heart too full
Of love for you to speak of aught besides!
Take your revenge, punish my odious passion;
Prove yourself worthy of your valiant sire,
And rid the world of an offensive monster!
Does Theseus' widow dare to love his son?
The frightful monster! Let her not escape you!
Here is my heart. This is the place to strike.
Already prompt to expiate its guilt,
I feel it leap impatiently to meet
Your arm. Strike home. Or, if it would disgrace you
To steep your hand in such polluted blood,
If that were punishment too mild to slake
Your hatred, lend me then your sword, if not
Your arm. Quick, give't.

Phaedra

OENONE
What, Madam, will you do?
Just gods! But someone comes. Go, fly from shame,
You cannot 'scape if seen by any thus.

SCENE VI
HIPPOLYTUS, THERAMENES

THERAMENES
Is that the form of Phaedra that I see
Hurried away? What mean these signs of sorrow?
Where is your sword? Why are you pale, confused?

HIPPOLYTUS
Friend, let us fly. I am, indeed, confounded
With horror and astonishment extreme.
Phaedra—but no; gods, let this dreadful secret
Remain for ever buried in oblivion.

THERAMENES
The ship is ready if you wish to sail.
But Athens has already giv'n her vote;
Their leaders have consulted all her tribes;
Your brother is elected, Phaedra wins.

HIPPOLYTUS
Phaedra?

THERAMENES
A herald, charged with a commission
From Athens, has arrived to place the reins
Of power in her hands. Her son is King.

HIPPOLYTUS
Ye gods, who know her, do ye thus reward
Her virtue?

THERAMENES
A faint rumour meanwhile whispers
That Theseus is not dead, but in Epirus
Has shown himself. But, after all my search,
I know too well—

HIPPOLYTUS
Let nothing be neglected.
This rumour must be traced back to its source.

Phaedra

If it be found unworthy of belief,
Let us set sail, and cost whate'er it may,
To hands deserving trust the sceptre's sway.

ACT III

SCENE I
PHAEDRA, OENONE

PHAEDRA
Ah! Let them take elsewhere the worthless honours
They bring me. Why so urgent I should see them?
What flattering balm can soothe my wounded heart?
Far rather hide me: I have said too much.
My madness has burst forth like streams in flood,
And I have utter'd what should ne'er have reach'd
His ear. Gods! How he heard me! How reluctant
To catch my meaning, dull and cold as marble,
And eager only for a quick retreat!
How oft his blushes made my shame the deeper!
Why did you turn me from the death I sought?
Ah! When his sword was pointed to my bosom,
Did he grow pale, or try to snatch it from me?
That I had touch'd it was enough for him
To render it for ever horrible,
Leaving defilement on the hand that holds it.

OENONE
Thus brooding on your bitter disappointment,
You only fan a fire that must be stifled.
Would it not be more worthy of the blood
Of Minos to find peace in nobler cares,
And, in defiance of a wretch who flies
From what he hates, reign, mount the proffer'd throne?

PHAEDRA
I reign! Shall I the rod of empire sway,
When reason reigns no longer o'er myself?
When I have lost control of all my senses?
When 'neath a shameful yoke I scarce can breathe?
When I am dying?

OENONE
Fly.

Phaedra

PHAEDRA
I cannot leave him.

OENONE
Dare you not fly from him you dared to banish?

PHAEDRA
The time for that is past. He knows my frenzy.
I have o'erstepp'd the bounds of modesty,
And blazon'd forth my shame before his eyes.
Hope stole into my heart against my will.
Did you not rally my declining pow'rs?
Was it not you yourself recall'd my soul
When fluttering on my lips, and with your counsel,
Lent me fresh life, and told me I might love him?

OENONE
Blame me or blame me not for your misfortunes,
Of what was I incapable, to save you?
But if your indignation e'er was roused
By insult, can you pardon his contempt?
How cruelly his eyes, severely fix'd,
Survey'd you almost prostrate at his feet!
How hateful then appear'd his savage pride!
Why did not Phaedra see him then as I
Beheld him?

PHAEDRA
This proud mood that you resent
May yield to time. The rudeness of the forests
Where he was bred, inured to rigorous laws,
Clings to him still; love is a word he ne'er
Had heard before. It may be his surprise
Stunn'd him, and too much vehemence was shown
In all I said.

OENONE
Remember that his mother
Was a barbarian.

PHAEDRA
Scythian tho' she was,
She learned to love.

OENONE
He has for all the sex
Hatred intense.

PHAEDRA
Then in his heart no rival
Shall ever reign. Your counsel comes too late
Oenone, serve my madness, not my reason.
His heart is inaccessible to love.
Let us attack him where he has more feeling.
The charms of sovereignty appear'd to touch him;
He could not hide that he was drawn to Athens;
His vessels' prows were thither turn'd already,
All sail was set to scud before the breeze.
Go you on my behalf, to his ambition
Appeal, and let the prospect of the crown
Dazzle his eyes. The sacred diadem
Shall deck his brow, no higher honour mine
Than there to bind it. His shall be the pow'r
I cannot keep; and he shall teach my son
How to rule men. It may be he will deign
To be to him a father. Son and mother
He shall control. Try ev'ry means to move him;
Your words will find more favour than can mine.
Urge him with groans and tears; show Phaedra dying.
Nor blush to use the voice of supplication.
In you is my last hope; I'll sanction all
You say; and on the issue hangs my fate.

SCENE II

PHAEDRA (alone)
Venus implacable, who seest me shamed
And sore confounded, have I not enough
Been humbled? How can cruelty be stretch'd
Farther? Thy shafts have all gone home, and thou
Hast triumph'd. Would'st thou win a new renown?
Attack an enemy more contumacious:
Hippolytus neglects thee, braves thy wrath,
Nor ever at thine altars bow'd the knee.
Thy name offends his proud, disdainful ears.
Our interests are alike: avenge thyself,
Force him to love—
But what is this? Oenone
Return'd already? He detests me then,
And will not hear you.

SCENE III
PHAEDRA, OENONE

OENONE
Madam, you must stifle
A fruitless love. Recall your former virtue:
The king who was thought dead will soon appear
Before your eyes, Theseus has just arrived,
Theseus is here. The people flock to see him
With eager haste. I went by your command
To find the prince, when with a thousand shouts
The air was rent—

PHAEDRA
My husband is alive,
That is enough, Oenone. I have own'd
A passion that dishonours him. He lives:
I ask to know no more.

OENONE
What?

PHAEDRA
I foretold it,
But you refused to hear. Your tears prevail'd
Over my just remorse. Dying this morn,
I had deserved compassion; your advice
I took, and die dishonour'd.

OENONE
Die?

PHAEDRA
Just Heav'ns!
What have I done to-day? My husband comes,
With him his son: and I shall see the witness
Of my adulterous flame watch with what face
I greet his father, while my heart is big
With sighs he scorn'd, and tears that could not move him
Moisten mine eyes. Think you that his respect
For Theseus will induce him to conceal

My madness, nor disgrace his sire and king?
Will he be able to keep back the horror
He has for me? His silence would be vain.
I know my treason, and I lack the boldness
Of those abandon'd women who can taste
Tranquillity in crime, and show a forehead
All unabash'd. I recognize my madness,
Recall it all. These vaulted roofs, methinks,
These walls can speak, and, ready to accuse me,
Wait but my husband's presence to reveal
My perfidy. Death only can remove
This weight of horror. Is it such misfortune
To cease to live? Death causes no alarm
To misery. I only fear the name
That I shall leave behind me. For my sons
How sad a heritage! The blood of Jove
Might justly swell the pride that boasts descent
From Heav'n, but heavy weighs a mother's guilt
Upon her offspring. Yes, I dread the scorn
That will be cast on them, with too much truth,
For my disgrace. I tremble when I think
That, crush'd beneath that curse, they'll never dare
To raise their eyes.

OENONE
Doubt not I pity both;
Never was fear more just than yours. Why, then,
Expose them to this ignominy? Why
Will you accuse yourself? You thus destroy
The only hope that's left; it will be said
That Phaedra, conscious of her perfidy,
Fled from her husband's sight. Hippolytus
Will be rejoiced that, dying, you should lend
His charge support. What can I answer him?
He'll find it easy to confute my tale,
And I shall hear him with an air of triumph
To every open ear repeat your shame.
Sooner than that may fire from heav'n consume me!
Deceive me not. Say, do you love him still?
How look you now on this contemptuous prince?

PHAEDRA
As on a monster frightful to mine eyes.

OENONE
Why yield him, then, an easy victory?
You fear him? Venture to accuse him first,
As guilty of the charge which he may bring
This day against you. Who can say 'tis false?
All tells against him: in your hands his sword
Happily left behind, your present trouble,
Your past distress, your warnings to his father,
His exile which your earnest pray'rs obtain'd.

PHAEDRA
What! Would you have me slander innocence?

OENONE
My zeal has need of naught from you but silence.
Like you I tremble, and am loath to do it;
More willingly I'd face a thousand deaths,
But since without this bitter remedy
I lose you, and to me your life outweighs
All else, I'll speak. Theseus, howe'er enraged
Will do no worse than banish him again.
A father, when he punishes, remains
A father, and his ire is satisfied
With a light sentence. But if guiltless blood
Should flow, is not your honour of more moment?
A treasure far too precious to be risk'd?
You must submit, whatever it dictates;
For, when our reputation is at stake,
All must be sacrificed, conscience itself.
But someone comes. 'Tis Theseus.

PHAEDRA
And I see
Hippolytus, my ruin plainly written
In his stern eyes. Do what you will; I trust
My fate to you. I cannot help myself.

SCENE IV
THESEUS, HIPPOLYTUS, PHAEDRA, OENONE, THERAMENES

THESEUS
Fortune no longer fights against my wishes,
Madam, and to your arms restores—

PHAEDRA
Stay, Theseus!
Do not profane endearments that were once
So sweet, but which I am unworthy now
To taste. You have been wrong'd. Fortune has proved
Spiteful, nor in your absence spared your wife.
I am unfit to meet your fond caress,
How I may bear my shame my only care
Henceforth.

SCENE V
THESEUS, HIPPOLYTUS, THERAMENES

THESEUS
Strange welcome for your father, this!
What does it mean, my son?

HIPPOLYTUS
Phaedra alone
Can solve this mystery. But if my wish
Can move you, let me never see her more;
Suffer Hippolytus to disappear
For ever from the home that holds your wife.

THESEUS
You, my son! Leave me?

HIPPOLYTUS
'Twas not I who sought her:
'Twas you who led her footsteps to these shores.
At your departure you thought meet, my lord,
To trust Aricia and the Queen to this
Troezenian land, and I myself was charged
With their protection. But what cares henceforth
Need keep me here? My youth of idleness
Has shown its skill enough o'er paltry foes
That range the woods. May I not quit a life
Of such inglorious ease, and dip my spear
In nobler blood? Ere you had reach'd my age
More than one tyrant, monster more than one
Had felt the weight of your stout arm. Already,
Successful in attacking insolence,
You had removed all dangers that infested
Our coasts to east and west. The traveller fear'd
Outrage no longer. Hearing of your deeds,
Already Hercules relied on you,
And rested from his toils. While I, unknown
Son of so brave a sire, am far behind
Even my mother's footsteps. Let my courage
Have scope to act, and if some monster yet
Has 'scaped you, let me lay the glorious spoils

40

Down at your feet; or let the memory
Of death faced nobly keep my name alive,
And prove to all the world I was your son.

THESEUS
Why, what is this? What terror has possess'd
My family to make them fly before me?
If I return to find myself so fear'd,
So little welcome, why did Heav'n release me
From prison? My sole friend, misled by passion,
Was bent on robbing of his wife the tyrant
Who ruled Epirus. With regret I lent
The lover aid, but Fate had made us blind,
Myself as well as him. The tyrant seized me
Defenceless and unarm'd. Pirithous
I saw with tears cast forth to be devour'd
By savage beasts that lapp'd the blood of men.
Myself in gloomy caverns he inclosed,
Deep in the bowels of the earth, and nigh
To Pluto's realms. Six months I lay ere Heav'n
Had pity, and I 'scaped the watchful eyes
That guarded me. Then did I purge the world
Of a foul foe, and he himself has fed
His monsters. But when with expectant joy
To all that is most precious I draw near
Of what the gods have left me, when my soul
Looks for full satisfaction in a sight
So dear, my only welcome is a shudder,
Embrace rejected, and a hasty flight.
Inspiring, as I clearly do, such terror,
Would I were still a prisoner in Epirus!
Phaedra complains that I have suffer'd outrage.
Who has betray'd me? Speak. Why was I not
Avenged? Has Greece, to whom mine arm so oft
Brought useful aid, shelter'd the criminal?
You make no answer. Is my son, mine own
Dear son, confederate with mine enemies?
I'll enter. This suspense is overwhelming.
I'll learn at once the culprit and the crime,
And Phaedra must explain her troubled state.

SCENE VI
HIPPOLYTUS, THERAMENES

HIPPOLYTUS
What do these words portend, which seem'd to freeze
My very blood? Will Phaedra, in her frenzy
Accuse herself, and seal her own destruction?
What will the King say? Gods! What fatal poison
Has love spread over all his house! Myself,
Full of a fire his hatred disapproves,
How changed he finds me from the son he knew!
With dark forebodings in my mind alarm'd,
But innocence has surely naught to fear.
Come, let us go, and in some other place
Consider how I best may move my sire
To tenderness, and tell him of a flame
Vex'd but not vanquish'd by a father's blame.

ACT IV

SCENE I
THESEUS, OENONE

THESEUS
Ah! What is this I hear? Presumptuous traitor!
And would he have disgraced his father's honour?
With what relentless footsteps Fate pursues me!
Whither I go I know not, nor where know
I am. O kind affection ill repaid!
Audacious scheme! Abominable thought!
To reach the object of his foul desire
The wretch disdain'd not to use violence.
I know this sword that served him in his fury,
The sword I gave him for a nobler use.
Could not the sacred ties of blood restrain him?
And Phaedra, —was she loath to have him punish'd?
She held her tongue. Was that to spare the culprit?

OENONE
Nay, but to spare a most unhappy father.
O'erwhelm'd with shame that her eyes should have kindled
So infamous a flame and prompted him
To crime so heinous, Phaedra would have died.
I saw her raise her arm, and ran to save her.
To me alone you owe it that she lives;
And, in my pity both for her and you,
Have I against my will interpreted
Her tears.

THESEUS
The traitor! He might well turn pale.
'Twas fear that made him tremble when he saw me.
I was astonish'd that he show'd no pleasure;
His frigid greeting chill'd my tenderness.
But was this guilty passion that devours him
Declared already ere I banish'd him
From Athens?

OENONE
Sire, remember how the Queen
Urged you. Illicit love caused all her hatred.

THESEUS
And then this fire broke out again at Troezen?

OENONE
Sire, I have told you all. Too long the Queen
Has been allow'd to bear her grief alone
Let me now leave you and attend to her.

SCENE II
THESEUS, HIPPOLYTUS

THESEUS
Ah! There he is. Great gods! That noble mien
Might well deceive an eye less fond than mine!
Why should the sacred stamp of virtue gleam
Upon the forehead of an impious wretch?
Ought not the blackness of a traitor's heart
To show itself by sure and certain signs?

HIPPOLYTUS
My father, may I ask what fatal cloud
Has troubled your majestic countenance?
Dare you not trust this secret to your son?

THESEUS
Traitor, how dare you show yourself before me?
Monster, whom Heaven's bolts have spared too long!
Survivor of that robber crew whereof
I cleansed the earth. After your brutal lust
Scorn'd even to respect my marriage bed,
You venture—you, my hated foe—to come
Into my presence, here, where all is full
Of your foul infamy, instead of seeking
Some unknown land that never heard my name.
Fly, traitor, fly! Stay not to tempt the wrath
That I can scarce restrain, nor brave my hatred.
Disgrace enough have I incurr'd for ever
In being father of so vile a son,
Without your death staining indelibly
The glorious record of my noble deeds.
Fly, and unless you wish quick punishment
To add you to the criminals cut off
By me, take heed this sun that lights us now
Ne'er sees you more set foot upon this soil.
I tell you once again, —fly, haste, return not,
Rid all my realms of your atrocious presence.
To thee, to thee, great Neptune, I appeal
If erst I clear'd thy shores of foul assassins
Recall thy promise to reward those efforts,

Phaedra

Crown'd with success, by granting my first pray'r.
Confined for long in close captivity,
I have not yet call'd on thy pow'rful aid,
Sparing to use the valued privilege
Till at mine utmost need. The time is come
I ask thee now. Avenge a wretched father!
I leave this traitor to thy wrath; in blood
Quench his outrageous fires, and by thy fury
Theseus will estimate thy favour tow'rds him.

HIPPOLYTUS
Phaedra accuses me of lawless passion!
This crowning horror all my soul confounds;
Such unexpected blows, falling at once,
O'erwhelm me, choke my utterance, strike me dumb.

THESEUS
Traitor, you reckon'd that in timid silence
Phaedra would bury your brutality.
You should not have abandon'd in your flight
The sword that in her hands helps to condemn you;
Or rather, to complete your perfidy,
You should have robb'd her both of speech and life.

HIPPOLYTUS
Justly indignant at a lie so black
I might be pardon'd if I told the truth;
But it concerns your honour to conceal it.
Approve the reverence that shuts my mouth;
And, without wishing to increase your woes,
Examine closely what my life has been.
Great crimes are never single, they are link'd
To former faults. He who has once transgress'd
May violate at last all that men hold
Most sacred; vice, like virtue, has degrees
Of progress; innocence was never seen
To sink at once into the lowest depths
Of guilt. No virtuous man can in a day
Turn traitor, murderer, an incestuous wretch.
The nursling of a chaste, heroic mother,
I have not proved unworthy of my birth.
Pittheus, whose wisdom is by all esteem'd,
Deign'd to instruct me when I left her hands.

Phaedra

It is no wish of mine to vaunt my merits,
But, if I may lay claim to any virtue,
I think beyond all else I have display'd
Abhorrence of those sins with which I'm charged.
For this Hippolytus is known in Greece,
So continent that he is deem'd austere.
All know my abstinence inflexible:
The daylight is not purer than my heart.
How, then, could I, burning with fire profane—

THESEUS
Yes, dastard, 'tis that very pride condemns you.
I see the odious reason of your coldness
Phaedra alone bewitch'd your shameless eyes;
Your soul, to others' charms indifferent,
Disdain'd the blameless fires of lawful love.

HIPPOLYTUS
No, father, I have hidden it too long,
This heart has not disdain'd a sacred flame.
Here at your feet I own my real offence:
I love, and love in truth where you forbid me;
Bound to Aricia by my heart's devotion,
The child of Pallas has subdued your son.
A rebel to your laws, her I adore,
And breathe forth ardent sighs for her alone.

THESEUS
You love her? Heav'ns!
But no, I see the trick.
You feign a crime to justify yourself.

HIPPOLYTUS
Sir, I have shunn'd her for six months, and still
Love her. To you yourself I came to tell it,
Trembling the while. Can nothing clear your mind
Of your mistake? What oath can reassure you?
By heav'n and earth and all the pow'rs of nature—

THESEUS
The wicked never shrink from perjury.
Cease, cease, and spare me irksome protestations,
If your false virtue has no other aid.

47

Phaedra

HIPPOLYTUS
Tho' it to you seem false and insincere,
Phaedra has secret cause to know it true.

THESEUS
Ah! how your shamelessness excites my wrath!

HIPPOLYTUS
What is my term and place of banishment?

THESEUS
Were you beyond the Pillars of Alcides,
Your perjured presence were too near me yet.

HIPPOLYTUS
What friends will pity me, when you forsake
And think me guilty of a crime so vile?

THESEUS
Go, look you out for friends who hold in honour
Adultery and clap their hands at incest,
Low, lawless traitors, steep'd in infamy,
The fit protectors of a knave like you.

HIPPOLYTUS
Are incest and adultery the words
You cast at me? I hold my tongue. Yet think
What mother Phaedra had; too well you know
Her blood, not mine, is tainted with those horrors.

THESEUS
What! Does your rage before my eyes lose all
Restraint? For the last time, —out of my sight!
Hence, traitor! Wait not till a father's wrath
Force thee away 'mid general execration.

SCENE III

THESEUS (alone)
Wretch! Thou must meet inevitable ruin.
Neptune has sworn by Styx—to gods themselves
A dreadful oath, —and he will execute
His promise. Thou canst not escape his vengeance.
I loved thee; and, in spite of thine offence,
My heart is troubled by anticipation
For thee. But thou hast earn'd thy doom too well.
Had father ever greater cause for rage?
Just gods, who see the grief that overwhelms me,
Why was I cursed with such a wicked son?

SCENE IV
PHAEDRA, THESEUS

PHAEDRA
My lord, I come to you, fill'd with just dread.
Your voice raised high in anger reach'd mine ears,
And much I fear that deeds have follow'd threats.
Oh, if there yet is time, spare your own offspring.
Respect your race and blood, I do beseech you.
Let me not hear that blood cry from the ground;
Save me the horror and perpetual pain
Of having caused his father's hand to shed it.

THESEUS
No, Madam, from that stain my hand is free.
But, for all that, the wretch has not escaped me.
The hand of an Immortal now is charged
With his destruction. 'Tis a debt that Neptune
Owes me, and you shall be avenged.

PHAEDRA
A debt
Owed you? Pray'rs made in anger —

THESEUS
Never fear
That they will fail. Rather join yours to mine
In all their blackness paint for me his crimes,
And fan my tardy passion to white heat.
But yet you know not all his infamy;
His rage against you overflows in slanders;
Your mouth, he says, is full of all deceit,
He says Aricia has his heart and soul,
That her alone he loves.

PHAEDRA
Aricia?

THESEUS
Aye,
He said it to my face! an idle pretext!

Phaedra

A trick that gulls me not! Let us hope Neptune
Will do him speedy justice. To his altars
I go, to urge performance of his oaths.

SCENE V

PHAEDRA (alone)
Ah, he is gone! What tidings struck mine ears?
What fire, half smother'd, in my heart revives?
What fatal stroke falls like a thunderbolt?
Stung by remorse that would not let me rest,
I tore myself out of Oenone's arms,
And flew to help Hippolytus with all
My soul and strength. Who knows if that repentance
Might not have moved me to accuse myself?
And, if my voice had not been choked with shame,
Perhaps I had confess'd the frightful truth.
Hippolytus can feel, but not for me!
Aricia has his heart, his plighted troth.
Ye gods, when, deaf to all my sighs and tears,
He arm'd his eye with scorn, his brow with threats,
I deem'd his heart, impregnable to love,
Was fortified 'gainst all my sex alike.
And yet another has prevail'd to tame
His pride, another has secured his favour.
Perhaps he has a heart easily melted;
I am the only one he cannot bear!
And shall I charge myself with his defence?

Phaedra

SCENE VI
PHAEDRA, OENONE

PHAEDRA
Know you, dear Nurse, what I have learn'd just now?

OENONE
No; but I come in truth with trembling limbs.
I dreaded with what purpose you went forth,
The fear of fatal madness made me pale.

PHAEDRA
Who would have thought it, Nurse? I had a rival.

OENONE
A rival?

PHAEDRA
Yes, he loves. I cannot doubt it.
This wild untamable Hippolytus,
Who scorn'd to be admired, whom lovers' sighs
Wearied, this tiger, whom I fear'd to rouse,
Fawns on a hand that has subdued his pride:
Aricia has found entrance to his heart.

OENONE
Aricia?

PHAEDRA
Ah! anguish as yet untried!
For what new tortures am I still reserved?
All I have undergone, transports of passion,
Longings and fears, the horrors of remorse,
The shame of being spurn'd with contumely,
Were feeble foretastes of my present torments.
They love each other! By what secret charm
Have they deceived me? Where, and when, and how
Met they? You knew it all. Why was I cozen'd?
You never told me of those stolen hours
Of amorous converse. Have they oft been seen
Talking together? Did they seek the shades

53

Phaedra

Of thickest woods? Alas! full freedom had they
To see each other. Heav'n approved their sighs;
They loved without the consciousness of guilt;
And every morning's sun for them shone clear,
While I, an outcast from the face of Nature,
Shunn'd the bright day, and sought to hide myself.
Death was the only god whose aid I dared
To ask: I waited for the grave's release.
Water'd with tears, nourish'd with gall, my woe
Was all too closely watch'd; I did not dare
To weep without restraint. In mortal dread
Tasting this dangerous solace, I disguised
My terror 'neath a tranquil countenance,
And oft had I to check my tears, and smile.

OENONE
What fruit will they enjoy of their vain love?
They will not see each other more.

PHAEDRA
That love
Will last for ever. Even while I speak,
Ah, fatal thought, they laugh to scorn the madness
Of my distracted heart. In spite of exile
That soon must part them, with a thousand oaths
They seal yet closer union. Can I suffer
A happiness, Oenone, which insults me?
I crave your pity. She must be destroy'd.
My husband's wrath against a hateful stock
Shall be revived, nor must the punishment
Be light: the sister's guilt passes the brothers'.
I will entreat him in my jealous rage.
What am I saying? Have I lost my senses?
Is Phaedra jealous, and will she implore
Theseus for help? My husband lives, and yet
I burn. For whom? Whose heart is this I claim
As mine? At every word I say, my hair
Stands up with horror. Guilt henceforth has pass'd
All bounds. Hypocrisy and incest breathe
At once thro' all. My murderous hands are ready
To spill the blood of guileless innocence.
Do I yet live, wretch that I am, and dare
To face this holy Sun from whom I spring?

My father's sire was king of all the gods;
My ancestors fill all the universe.
Where can I hide? In the dark realms of Pluto?
But there my father holds the fatal urn;
His hand awards th' irrevocable doom:
Minos is judge of all the ghosts in hell.
Ah! how his awful shade will start and shudder
When he shall see his daughter brought before him,
Forced to confess sins of such varied dye,
Crimes it may be unknown to hell itself!
What wilt thou say, my father, at a sight
So dire? I think I see thee drop the urn,
And, seeking some unheard-of punishment,
Thyself become my executioner.
Spare me! A cruel goddess has destroy'd
Thy race; and in my madness recognize
Her wrath. Alas! My aching heart has reap'd
No fruit of pleasure from the frightful crime
The shame of which pursues me to the grave,
And ends in torment life-long misery.

OENONE
Ah, Madam, pray dismiss a groundless dread:
Look less severely on a venial error.
You love. We cannot conquer destiny.
You were drawn on as by a fatal charm.
Is that a marvel without precedent
Among us? Has love triumph'd over you,
And o'er none else? Weakness is natural
To man. A mortal, to a mortal's lot
Submit. You chafe against a yoke that others
Have long since borne. The dwellers in Olympus,
The gods themselves, who terrify with threats
The sins of men, have burn'd with lawless fires.

PHAEDRA
What words are these I hear? What counsel this
You dare to give me? Will you to the end
Pour poison in mine ears? You have destroy'd me.
You brought me back when I should else have quitted
The light of day, made me forget my duty
And see Hippolytus, till then avoided.
What hast thou done? Why did your wicked mouth

Phaedra

With blackest lies slander his blameless life?
Perhaps you've slain him, and the impious pray'r
Of an unfeeling father has been answer'd.
No, not another word! Go, hateful monster;
Away, and leave me to my piteous fate.
May Heav'n with justice pay you your deserts!
And may your punishment for ever be
A terror to all those who would, like you,
Nourish with artful wiles the weaknesses
Of princes, push them to the brink of ruin
To which their heart inclines, and smooth the path
Of guilt. Such flatterers doth the wrath of Heav'n
Bestow on kings as its most fatal gift.

OENONE (alone)
O gods! to serve her what have I not done?
This is the due reward that I have won.

ACT V

SCENE I
HIPPOLYTUS, ARICIA

ARICIA
Can you keep silent in this mortal peril?
Your father loves you. Will you leave him thus
Deceived? If in your cruel heart you scorn
My tears, content to see me nevermore,
Go, part from poor Aricia; but at least,
Going, secure the safety of your life.
Defend your honor from a shameful stain,
And force your father to recall his pray'rs.
There yet is time. Why out of mere caprice
Leave the field free to Phaedra's calumnies?
Let Theseus know the truth.

HIPPOLYTUS
Could I say more,
Without exposing him to dire disgrace?
How should I venture, by revealing all,
To make a father's brow grow red with shame?
The odious mystery to you alone
Is known. My heart has been outpour'd to none
Save you and Heav'n. I could not hide from you
(Judge if I love you), all I fain would hide
E'en from myself. But think under what seal
I spoke. Forget my words, if that may be;
And never let so pure a mouth disclose
This dreadful secret. Let us trust to Heav'n
My vindication, for the gods are just;
For their own honour will they clear the guiltless;
Sooner or later punish'd for her crime,
Phaedra will not escape the shame she merits.
I ask no other favour than your silence;
In all besides I give my wrath free scope.
Make your escape from this captivity,
Be bold to bear me company in flight;
Linger not here on this accursed soil,

Where virtue breathes a pestilential air.
To cover your departure take advantage
Of this confusion, caused by my disgrace.
The means of flight are ready, be assured;
You have as yet no other guards than mine.
Pow'rful defenders will maintain our quarrel;
Argos spreads open arms, and Sparta calls us.
Let us appeal for justice to our friends,
Nor suffer Phaedra, in a common ruin
Joining us both, to hunt us from the throne,
And aggrandise her son by robbing us.
Embrace this happy opportunity:
What fear restrains? You seem to hesitate.
Your interest alone prompts me to urge
Boldness. When I am all on fire, how comes it
That you are ice? Fear you to follow then
A banish'd man?

ARICIA
Ah, dear to me would be
Such exile! With what joy, my fate to yours
United, could I live, by all the world
Forgotten! but not yet has that sweet tie
Bound us together. How then can I steal
Away with you? I know the strictest honour
Forbids me not out of your father's hands
To free myself; this is no parent's home,
And flight is lawful when one flies from tyrants.
But you, Sir, love me; and my virtue shrinks —

HIPPOLYTUS
No, no, your reputation is to me
As dear as to yourself. A nobler purpose
Brings me to you. Fly from your foes, and follow
A husband. Heav'n, that sends us these misfortunes,
Sets free from human instruments the pledge
Between us. Torches do not always light
The face of Hymen.
At the gates of Troezen,
'Mid ancient tombs where princes of my race
Lie buried, stands a temple, ne'er approach'd
By perjurers, where mortals dare not make
False oaths, for instant punishment befalls

Phaedra

The guilty. Falsehood knows no stronger check
Than what is present there—the fear of death
That cannot be avoided. Thither then
We'll go, if you consent, and swear to love
For ever, take the guardian god to witness
Our solemn vows, and his paternal care
Entreat. I will invoke the name of all
The holiest Pow'rs; chaste Dian, and the Queen
Of Heav'n, yea all the gods who know my heart
Will guarantee my sacred promises.

ARICIA
The King draws near. Depart, —make no delay.
To mask my flight, I linger yet one moment.
Go you; and leave with me some trusty guide,
To lead my timid footsteps to your side.

SCENE II
THESEUS, ARICIA, ISMENE

THESEUS
Ye gods, throw light upon my troubled mind,
Show me the truth which I am seeking here.

ARICIA (aside to ISMENE)
Get ready, dear Ismene, for our flight.

SCENE III
THESEUS, ARICIA

THESEUS
Your colour comes and goes, you seem confused,
Madame! What business had my son with you?

ARICIA
Sire, he was bidding me farewell for ever.

THESEUS
Your eyes, it seems, can tame that stubborn pride;
And the first sighs he breathes are paid to you.

ARICIA
I can't deny the truth; he has not, Sire,
Inherited your hatred and injustice;
He did not treat me like a criminal.

THESEUS
That is to say, he swore eternal love.
Do not rely on that inconstant heart;
To others has he sworn as much before.

ARICIA
He, Sire?

THESEUS
You ought to check his roving taste.
How could you bear a partnership so vile?

ARICIA
And how can you endure that vilest slanders
Should make a life so pure as black as pitch?
Have you so little knowledge of his heart?
Do you so ill distinguish between guilt
And innocence? What mist before your eyes
Blinds them to virtue so conspicuous?
Ah! 'tis too much to let false tongues defame him.
Repent; call back your murderous wishes, Sire;
Fear, fear lest Heav'n in its severity

Hate you enough to hear and grant your pray'rs.
Oft in their wrath the gods accept our victims,
And oftentimes chastise us with their gifts.

THESEUS
No, vainly would you cover up his guilt.
Your love is blind to his depravity.
But I have witness irreproachable:
Tears have I seen, true tears, that may be trusted.

ARICIA
Take heed, my lord. Your hands invincible
Have rid the world of monsters numberless;
But all are not destroy'd, one you have left
Alive—Your son forbids me to say more.
Knowing with what respect he still regards you,
I should too much distress him if I dared
Complete my sentence. I will imitate
His reverence, and, to keep silence, leave you.

SCENE IV

THESEUS (alone)
What is there in her mind? What meaning lurks
In speech begun but to be broken short?
Would both deceive me with a vain pretence?
Have they conspired to put me to the torture?
And yet, despite my stern severity,
What plaintive voice cries deep within my heart?
A secret pity troubles and alarms me.
Oenone shall be questioned once again,
I must have clearer light upon this crime.
Guards, bid Oenone come, and come alone.

SCENE V
THESEUS, PANOPE

PANOPE
I know not what the Queen intends to do,
But from her agitation dread the worst.
Fatal despair is painted on her features;
Death's pallor is already in her face.
Oenone, shamed and driven from her sight,
Has cast herself into the ocean depths.
None knows what prompted her to deed so rash;
And now the waves hide her from us for ever.

THESEUS
What say you?

PANOPE
Her sad fate seems to have added
Fresh trouble to the Queen's tempestuous soul.
Sometimes, to soothe her secret pain, she clasps
Her children close, and bathes them with her tears;
Then suddenly, the mother's love forgotten,
She thrusts them from her with a look of horror,
She wanders to and fro with doubtful steps;
Her vacant eye no longer knows us. Thrice
She wrote, and thrice did she, changing her mind,
Destroy the letter ere 'twas well begun.
Vouchsafe to see her, Sire: vouchsafe to help her.

THESEUS
Heav'ns! Is Oenone dead, and Phaedra bent
On dying too? Oh, call me back my son!
Let him defend himself, and I am ready
To hear him. Be not hasty to bestow
Thy fatal bounty, Neptune; let my pray'rs
Rather remain ever unheard. Too soon
I lifted cruel hands, believing lips
That may have lied! Ah! What despair may follow!

SCENE VI
THESEUS, THERAMENES

THESEUS
Theramenes, is't thou? Where is my son?
I gave him to thy charge from tenderest childhood.
But whence these tears that overflow thine eyes?
How is it with my son?

THERAMENES
Concern too late!
Affection vain! Hippolytus is dead.

THESEUS
Gods!

THERAMENES
I have seen the flow'r of all mankind
Cut off, and I am bold to say that none
Deserved it less.

THESEUS
What! My son dead! When I
Was stretching out my arms to him, has Heav'n
Hasten'd his end? What was this sudden stroke?

THERAMENES
Scarce had we pass'd out of the gates of Troezen,
He silent in his chariot, and his guards
Downcast and silent too, around him ranged;
To the Mycenian road he turn'd his steeds,
Then, lost in thought, allow'd the reins to lie
Loose on their backs. His noble chargers, erst
So full of ardour to obey his voice,
With head depress'd and melancholy eye
Seem'd now to mark his sadness and to share it.
A frightful cry, that issues from the deep,
With sudden discord rends the troubled air;
And from the bosom of the earth a groan
Is heard in answer to that voice of terror.
Our blood is frozen at our very hearts;

Phaedra

With bristling manes the list'ning steeds stand still.
Meanwhile upon the watery plain there rises
A mountain billow with a mighty crest
Of foam, that shoreward rolls, and, as it breaks
Before our eyes vomits a furious monster.
With formidable horns its brow is arm'd,
And all its body clothed with yellow scales,
In front a savage bull, behind a dragon
Turning and twisting in impatient rage.
Its long continued bellowings make the shore
Tremble; the sky seems horror-struck to see it;
The earth with terror quakes; its poisonous breath
Infects the air. The wave that brought it ebbs
In fear. All fly, forgetful of the courage
That cannot aid, and in a neighbouring temple
Take refuge—all save bold Hippolytus.
A hero's worthy son, he stays his steeds,
Seizes his darts, and, rushing forward, hurls
A missile with sure aim that wounds the monster
Deep in the flank. With rage and pain it springs
E'en to the horses' feet, and, roaring, falls,
Writhes in the dust, and shows a fiery throat
That covers them with flames, and blood, and smoke.
Fear lends them wings; deaf to his voice for once,
And heedless of the curb, they onward fly.
Their master wastes his strength in efforts vain;
With foam and blood each courser's bit is red.
Some say a god, amid this wild disorder,
Was seen with goads pricking their dusty flanks.
O'er jagged rocks they rush urged on by terror;
Crash! goes the axle-tree. Th' intrepid youth
Sees his car broken up, flying to pieces;
He falls himself entangled in the reins.
Pardon my grief. That cruel spectacle
Will be for me a source of endless tears.
I saw thy hapless son, I saw him, Sire,
Drag'd by the horses that his hands had fed,
Pow'rless to check their fierce career, his voice
But adding to their fright, his body soon
One mass of wounds. Our cries of anguish fill
The plain. At last they slacken their swift pace,
Then stop, not far from those old tombs that mark
Where lie the ashes of his royal sires.

Phaedra

Panting I thither run, and after me
His guard, along the track stain'd with fresh blood
That reddens all the rocks; caught in the briers
Locks of his hair hang dripping, gory spoils!
I come, I call him. Stretching forth his hand,
He opens his dying eyes, soon closed again.
"The gods have robb'd me of a guiltless life, "
I hear him say: "Take care of sad Aricia
When I am dead. Dear friend, if e'er my father
Mourn, undeceived, his son's unhappy fate
Falsely accused; to give my spirit peace,
Tell him to treat his captive tenderly,
And to restore—" With that the hero's breath
Fails, and a mangled corpse lies in my arms,
A piteous object, trophy of the wrath
Of Heav'n—so changed, his father would not know him.

THESEUS
Alas, my son! Dear hope for ever lost!
The ruthless gods have served me but too well.
For what a life of anguish and remorse
Am I reserved!

THERAMENES
Aricia at that instant,
Flying from you, comes timidly, to take him
For husband, there, in presence of the gods.
Thus drawing nigh, she sees the grass all red
And reeking, sees (sad sight for lover's eye!)
Hippolytus stretch'd there, pale and disfigured.
But, for a time doubtful of her misfortune,
Unrecognized the hero she adores,
She looks, and asks—"Where is Hippolytus? "
Only too sure at last that he lies there
Before her, with sad eyes that silently
Reproach the gods, she shudders, groans, and falls
Swooning and all but lifeless, at his feet.
Ismene, all in tears, kneels down beside her,
And calls her back to life—life that is naught
But sense of pain. And I, to whom this light
Is darkness now, come to discharge the duty
The hero has imposed on me, to tell thee
His last request—a melancholy task.

Phaedra

But hither comes his mortal enemy.

Phaedra

SCENE VII
THESEUS, PHAEDRA, THERAMENES, PANOPE, GUARDS

THESEUS
Madame, you've triumph'd, and my son is kill'd!
Ah, but what room have I for fear! How justly
Suspicion racks me that in blaming him
I err'd! But he is dead; accept your victim;
Rightly or wrongly slain, let your heart leap
For joy. My eyes shall be for ever blind:
Since you accuse him, I'll believe him guilty.
His death affords me cause enough for tears,
Without a foolish search for further light
Which, pow'rless to restore him to my grief,
Might only serve to make me more unhappy,
Far from this shore and far from you I'll fly,
For here the image of my mangled son
Would haunt my memory and drive me mad.
From the whole world I fain would banish me,
For all the world seems to rise up in judgment
Against me; and my very glory weights
My punishment; for, were my name less known
'Twere easier to hide me. All the favours
The gods have granted me I mourn and hate,
Nor will I importune them with vain pray'rs
Henceforth for ever. Give me what they may,
What they have taken will all else outweigh.

PHAEDRA
Theseus, I cannot hear you and keep silence:
I must repair the wrong that he has suffer'd—
Your son was innocent.

THESEUS
Unhappy father!
And it was on your word that I condemn'd him!
Think you such cruelty can be excused—

PHAEDRA
Moments to me are precious; hear me, Theseus.
'Twas I who cast an eye of lawless passion

69

On chaste and dutiful Hippolytus.
Heav'n in my bosom kindled baleful fire,
And vile Oenone's cunning did the rest.
She fear'd Hippolytus, knowing my madness,
Would make that passion known which he regarded
With horror; so advantage of my weakness
She took, and hasten'd to accuse him first.
For that she has been punish'd, tho' too mildly;
Seeking to shun my wrath she cast herself
Beneath the waves. The sword ere now had cut
My thread of life, but slander'd innocence
Made its cry heard, and I resolved to die
In a more lingering way, confessing first
My penitence to you. A poison, brought
To Athens by Medea, runs thro' my veins.
Already in my heart the venom works,
Infusing there a strange and fatal chill;
Already as thro' thickening mists I see
The spouse to whom my presence is an outrage;
Death, from mine eyes veiling the light of heav'n,
Restores its purity that they defiled.

PANOPE
She dies my lord!

THESEUS
Would that the memory
Of her disgraceful deed could perish with her!
Ah, disabused too late! Come, let us go,
And with the blood of mine unhappy son
Mingle our tears, clasping his dear remains,
In deep repentance for a pray'r detested.
Let him be honour'd as he well deserves;
And, to appease his sore offended ghost,
Be her near kinsmen's guilt whate'er it may,
Aricia shall be held my daughter from to-day.

Printed in the United States
121033LV00006B/152/A

9 781406 542066